WHY "RELIGION" HAS NOT DIED OFF

AND THANK "GODNESS" SHOULD NOT

S JAEGER

ReEnvision Press

INTRODUCTION

This book draws upon a number of my life experiences and my upbringing in general, with regard to spirituality....

I was raised my first four years by my grandparents, who were immigrants from Ukraine and Poland (grandfather and grandmother, respectively). My grandfather followed the ideas of The Mennonites, and my grandmother, The Baptists.

When my mother came to America at the age of twelve, after World War II was over - to Ellis Island - she soon joined an ethnic German-speaking Baptist church, married at the age of twenty, and my father immediately pursued training in the field of Christian ministry.

A t first, my parents had strongly considered becoming missionaries in Canada, and while this was not ultimately pursued, my father did complete an undergraduate degree from Detroit Bible College. They were particularly oriented toward the Plymouth Brethren approach, and I was thus brought up for a time, as a Plymouth Brethren - something not too far akin to the Mennonites, in certain ways.

At the age of 21, I spent a week at a training center known as

LaBri, near Boston, Massachusetts. This was the American version of what had been originally started in Switzerland by Francis Schaefer: a group dedicated to strongly pursuing Christian faith from a more intellectual (aka thinking) perspective.

———

In later years, I found myself taking up some assistance from two non-"spiritual" sources: psychoanalysts, both physicians; one, of no faith, and the other, a Jewish man: the former, originally from California, and the other, actually living in California at the time I sought their advice. I also received assistance in the Cognitive Therapy approach, and later, also explored meditation and Buddhism.

And while living in California for a few years in my twenties, I would hike, and also do some traveling in Arizona, where I spent some time on the Navajo Indian Reservation, to include the Indian groups around Flagstaff and Holbrook. And I then started collecting what would be a number of books on Indians and Indian herbal medicine.

———

Now, in 2021, I finally reignited my interest in the Native Americans, by visiting the Cherokee Indian areas of Cherokee, North Carolina, and Vonore, Tennessee.

———

Now, I might also mention that I spent two decades living in a town which was immensely oriented to teaching Christian leaders.

———

This book was written in the Fall of 2021, while I camped at the Cherokee National Forest, what with my exploring the the Native American Indians nearby - specifically, The Cherokees, on a trip to that Tennessee area once known as a major settlement of the Cherokee Indians: Monroe County, Tennessee, where it said that "countless Overhill Cherokee towns are buried under water in East Tennessee." (fernwehtun.com).

I stayed three days, camping by night in that nearby Cherokee National Forest, which is located in the Southern Appalachian Mountains of East Tennessee. This 650,000-acre forest is the "largest tract of public land in Tennessee and adjoins other national forests in Virginia, North Carolina and Georgia." (fs.usda.gov)

The rough draft for this book was written while in a tent, one night: a hunter's blind, to be exact. Fitting for the life of discussing Indian ways?

During this trip, I visited Fort Loudon State Historic Site & Park, in Vonore, Tennessee, part of Monroe County, a fort originally "constructed in 1756 and served as a military garrison for less than five years. The Cherokee eventually realized they had been betrayed outside of the Fort, so they captured and burned it down." (fernwehtun.com).

I also visited and was greatly inspired by nearby Sequoyah Birthplace Museum.

As for Sequoyah: "when he [Sequoyah] was a soldier, Sequoyah spent a lot of time thinking about how his fellow Cherokee could not write home, read (especially war-related news and military orders), or document anything about their lives like the European settlers.... Sequoyah proposed the idea of developing a Cherokee alphabet and written language, which his friends and family ridiculed him for.

Many sources say his wife constantly sabotaged his work and discouraged him from continuing. After twelve long years, and with unwavering support from his daughter, Sequoyah finished his syllabary and began teaching others how to use it." (fernwehtun.com)

———

Presently, I also do considerable traveling in Appalachian Kentucky, and have also been exploring the Appalachian parts of Tennessee, West Virginia, and North Carolina, having visited The Appalachian Museum in Clinton, Tennessee twice now - both times in the past six months. A most fascinating place.

Amongst the parts of *Kentucky* I have greatly explored are the counties of Casey County - known for its strong presence of both the Amish and Mennonites, and Lincoln and Russell counties, too, as well as areas in and around Morehead and Campton and West Liberty. And have also explored Harlan, Kentucky, on a three-day fact-finding trip. Lately I have spent considerable time exploring areas around London and Somerset, Kentucky.

———

I might mention that I twice lived in Berea, Kentucky - also part of Appalachia - for some four years - where where I lived as a townsperson and took some classes at Berea College as a non-degreee-pursuing community-based student, where I tutored there to pay back for the classes.

This book is a result of much reading, much discussing, and much thinking.... By a person who has no college degree .... But who has studied more in the areas of religion, science, mathematics, and more, than I can shake a stick at. An "autodidact" approach. And too, in the area of photography - where I spent some time studying with the New York Institute of Photography and have lots of self-teaching....

I do not claim to have The Answers - and I may well change some ideas here and there about this and that, as time goes on. But I bring up these thoughts for those interested - hoping they are good "food for thought", and my "best guess" at the present, about these matters. All to be taken as "hypotheses", not Gospel Truth.... For the day I have concluded I am certain of this and that, I will have become a God of sorts - and I'll be sure to let you know all about that ... in Triplicate....

CHAPTER 1

NEGATIVE CLAIMS ABOUT RELIGION(S)

NEGATIVE CLAIMS about Religion include the following:

1. That it is "Unscientific".

(Especially if one insists on seeing an Originator of the Universe as in a very, very specific manner that certainly rankles modern-day sensibilities - including those of a "scientific" bent):

.   .   .

That the Origination-Source has a Beard; and is White; and a Male; and Sits on a Throne. And His beard has a certain number of Whiskers; and that an Afterlife is only of a certain very specific manner, too, to include Walking on Marble - of a certain type and polish.

2. And, that this Originator, too, has a Vendetta against *certain* of those He created - but not others.

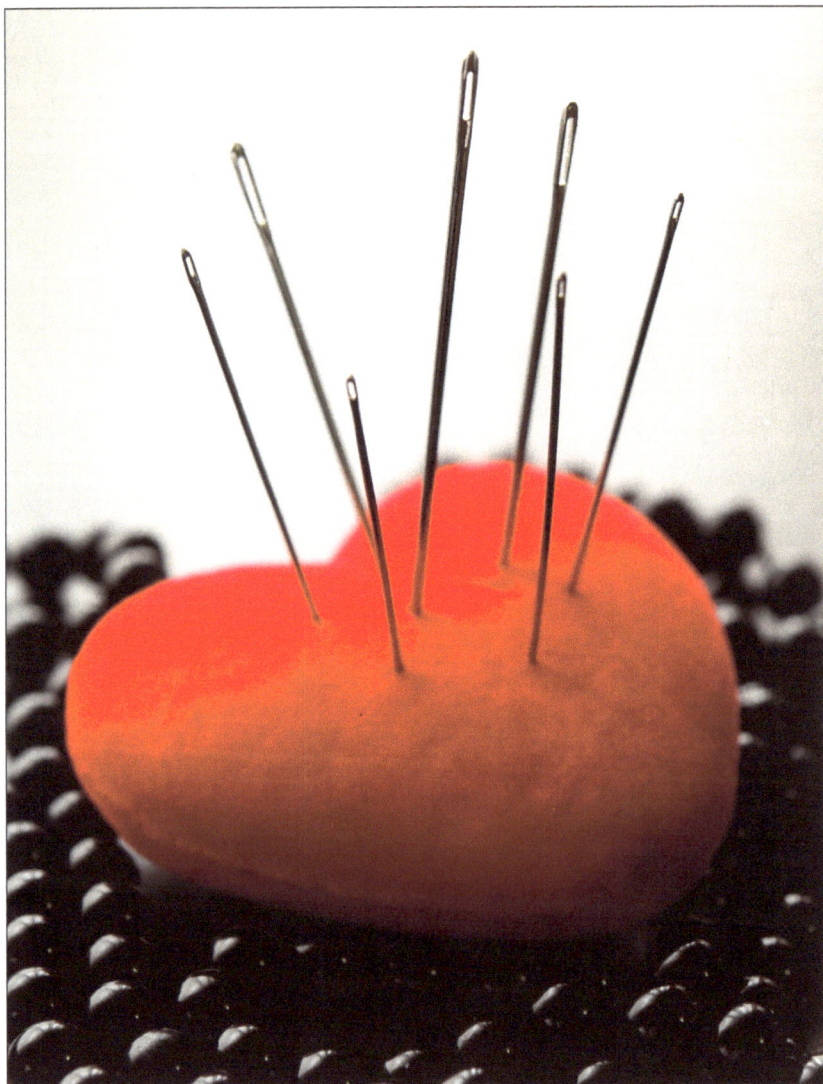

And that this is For the Greater Glory of God - or for the "Overall Best Welfare of the Universe": at least, in the long run.

Or to put it more clearly, that He Created *Junk* ("Sinners"), who have many flaws, particularly due to the limitations of his biological makeup, and yet, holds us "Accountable", nonetheless, for what ensues despite those Built-in limitations: and furthermore then, in most "Unloving" fashion, wants to - and does - Punish us : and with *delight*, too - for what we do not do or are - irrespective of us humans' having had no say in being Created (designed) WITH flaws (i.e. "sinners", as Christian scriptures term these flaws).

3. That (according to Karl Marx) "Religion is the Opiate of the Masses":

In other words, that it is a "Drug of Choice": a matter of a Collection-of-Defense-Mechanisms - to include a mass of Denials.

.   .   .

And furthermore, that even if this claim were entirely true, that there are, in Marx's opinion, far better ways to live:

Either, ways of living which involve the use of NO Defense Mechanism, or ones with far fewer "side effects". (But I do not necessarily believe that either have been proven to exist or be feasible.)

4. That many of its Claims are "Unprovable", and especially, that it makes "Unprovable"" Assumptions: "a priori" claims?

(*But this ignores, perhaps, that without a modicum of Assumptions - to include that we are Awake, not Asleep and merely Dreaming - or, that we are of Material Matter, not a bunch of One's and Zero's on a computer chip or computer board, we would hardly find life either of significance, or wish to go on - especially "when the Going Gets Rough".*)

5. That Religion(s) have brought nothing but war and other forms of suffering, and that Science will Bring a Better Way.

6. That *ALL TYPES* of Religion - and all of its Adherents - are The Exact Same:

To include, All of its Practitioners and all of its Leaders: including all of its Sages, and all its "pastors", and all of its Methods of helping Instill Wisdom (insights):
And ALL of its Views on Money.

And all of its views on Sex.

And all of its Views on free will vs determinism - and then, the related issue of whether we humans "deserve" punishment" or not - whether punishment, then, is only meant for the Betterment of Humanity, overall, by instilling a set of *"Boundaries"* with *"Teeth"* to them - to act as perhaps the only existing means of "encouraging" us to not "take shortcuts" for our own benefit - in other words, not to act expediently (in the short term, that is) for our happiness.

And as to whether it is used, say, to Aggrandize (some would term these individuals to be "Narcissistically-Religious persons);

Or, to use to Cover Up what amounts to a very *Expedient* (short-term-driven living), rather than for the "long haul" manner of living, which may involve more discomforts in the short term, such as the use of utterly-unnecessary violence, or lying.

Or, it may be used to try to Justify a manner of living which so many Non-Religious persons do in fact pursue; a life of use of Distractors and Security and "Grandness" (of self, and the Putting Down, at the same time, of Others), and even Revenge-Seeking.

(Such, perhaps, termed "Prosperity - Doctrine" Christians.)

Or, to accommodate an excessive fear of Death, and thus, and Insistence that the Overarching Import of Religion is to "Beat Death": or *as a lawyer once termed it, to me: to "Get Your Ticket Punched to Heaven"*.

To Ensure one Never Dies.

· · ·

Inasmuch as Many or Most people tend to be far too *Non*-Accepting of *Discomfort* - including its physical and emotional pains - that are of course tied to physical pains suffered all along Life's course, to include in Old Age - and the suffering, too, of the Loss of the Hope of Accomplishing all that one had hoped to, too: by Dying, that is: which does tend to "Throw a Monkey Wrench" into our Desires: our *Plans*.

And also inasmuch as we Humans then also tend to feel painful SHAME over our *incapacity* to *Transcend* our Limitations.

Especially, those limitations that are Built - In to us, by way of our limited lifespans, and our limited capacity to *remember* things, and too, the constraints of having to pursue our species' continuance, and all that this implies, especially our having a "sex drive": and then, all the compromises that this entails: to include a whole lot of labor of all sorts, and additional emotional sufferings in general; and many Moral Compromises often made, along the way, too, to try to acquire mates early on, and the "fittest ones", and best care for these mates and our young - our offspring, that is; and, by our brain's very architecture that is highly adapted to fear so many things - by way of our having an Amygdala, which is so very "trigger - happy" - so Reactive and so prone to reacting to our thwarted goals with not just fear, but Rage - and all that ensues: often in a most impulsive manner; in order to promote our Longevity and the creating of Offspring, hence ensuring the Longevity not just of ourselves but our race, too; and even the Longevity of our Planet, ultimately.

(And, this Rage producing not just Hatred and overall Non-Acceptance, but, also, an intense desire for "Revenge".)

———

Which can all too often take precedence over other aspects of most Religions, such as Happiness here and now - including the lessening of fears, and the helping others: irrespective of any Afterlife or not.

CHAPTER 2

THE FOLLOWING CHAPTERS OUTLINE THE BENEFITS OF "RELIGION"

THE FOLLOWING chapters or Topics are going to Outline the Benefits of "Religion": over that, too, of Alternate "Ways of Living".

Which arguably are their Own forms of Religion - only, not admitted to: see the Dogmatic Religion of "Atheists', to include Richard Dawkins, or see, too, the book by Ann Coulter.

CHAPTER 3

RELIGION IS A COUNTER TO AN EXCESSIVE CRAVING TO "PROVE" EVERYTHING

YES, I would maintain that the Alternative Forms of living are far, far more concerned - even "obsessed", if you will, with *proving* things.

And not just for the sake of Understanding or Justifying matters, but for the ultimate purpose of living in a most Dysfunctional manner: one that craves "Control", essentially. Predictability, if you will. And too, the avoidance of feeling shame over not "being in control": especially if one is shunned by many or all, over something or other, and finds oneself having to "live all alone in a room with their thoughts": their distressing ones, that is.

A manner of life that is essentially one of having an Addiction to Control: *to making Life utterly Predictable, in other words.*

And, too, to making life not just Predictable, but the making of Life to have Changes that are Slow-in-Coming: in other words, highly-adaptable-to, by way of these Changes happening Slowly, as opposed to overwhelming us with their pace of fluidity/change.

Because, as Humans, we do tend to find Sudden Changes to be most painful to deal with.

But alas, this Anti-Religious Over-focus on "Control" - call it "obsessive - compulsiveness", if one were an American Psychologist - having a markedly negative effect upon our Human Relations, our emotions (very much constricts them - and thus, our Joy and overall happiness, too), and our overall Efficiency level: wherein some Life Coach advisors urge us not to be "perfectionists", and instead adopt the approach of "80 percent equals Done".

Or, to put it as a Person who might have struggled with a substance issue such as excessive use of alcohol or certain "chemical" - based drugs, and who then gives up on "fixing" this, themselves, or through College-Solution Channels, aka "Therapy" or Psychoanalysis, and then turns, in desperation, to AA or NA (Alcoholics Anonymous or Narcotics Anonymous), the very first - and UTTERLY NECES-SARY/CRUCIAL TENET BEING, the RECOGNITION and ACCEPTANCE that WE CANNOT CONTROL things, and thus, CANNOT "CONTROL-AWAY" our SUFFERING.

Hence their phrase, "LET GO, and LET GOD".
(Wherein the Operative Element, in my opinion, not involving a Creator at all, ultimately, who is the Only Person IN Control: but rather, the acknowledgement that we are governed by Laws of the Universe, and THESE CANNOT be OVERRIDDEN.)

. . .

And thus, that WE CANNOT *OVERRIDE* - via SUPPOSEDLY "EXERCISING *CONTROL*" ("Willpower") these LAWS of the Universe.

(In other words, the successful utilizer of AA, or NA - or ANY RELIGION - involving an ACCEPTANCE that the VERY WORD "CONTROL" - and the so-called NOTION that we HAVE control - or can GET Control - is a FIGMENT of our IMAGINATION, and will, in time, NECESSARILY lead to MUCH EMOTIONAL *GRIEF*.)

CHAPTER 4

"RELIGION" HELPS US SEE THE OVERALL PICTURE

AND IT ESPECIALLY DOES THIS, perhaps, by insisting that Understanding - call it Wisdom, if you will - is not simply a matter of Mastering the insufferably huge number of Details in life - but rather, that it also and more-greatly involves "Seeing the Big Picture":

And this not accomplishable solely by use of "Logic": which is heavily oriented toward Details, vs. what is termed, sometimes derisively, as "Intuition".

Wherein there is the misconception that "Intuition" has only downsides (such as being "Unprovable", and too "Subjective", and too prone to being "Highjacked" by our Fears and our Cravings for a short-term Expedient manner of living, whereby what we might sometimes "see" and justify not with sheer logic, but "Intuition", ends up being Figments of our Imagination": or partly so.)

Sometimes then termed "psychosis", by Western Psychologists, or "Wishful Thinking". Or "delusions". Or "Limiting Beliefs". Or the having of a "psychotic break'.

But this utterly overlooking that what Intuition optimally involves, is a wholly different way of both Perceiving the Myriad of details (way too complex) that life presents us with - and in most utterly too rapid a fashion, too - and with far too few "labels" (words, aka "terms") to process such, with logic alone - especially if our vocabulary set is too "corrupted" with the attitudes of hate and blame.

Or too, if we lack the time and other tools to "refresh" our memories of just what we had once "figured out" (analyzed) using our logical faculties....

(For more information, a starter might be Brene' Brown's "The Gift of Imperfection".)

In short, that only Religion - or an environment rather free of "Education" - can provide an Alternative manner of Thinking: of dealing with Reality. Especially under certain conditions, environmentally, or when time constraints or stress are involved - including when our lives are in imminent danger.

CHAPTER 5

IT IS AN ALTERNATIVE WAY OF HANDLING OUR FEARS

IT THUS INVOLVES ADDRESSING our Core Fears not with the the ACQUIRING of THINGS (or the Acquiring of Stores of Money to GARNER Things), to include, then, their use as Distractors, or Controllers (often termed "Security"), or our Self-Aggrandizement and the Putting Down of Others (termed Status-Acquiring), and even the use of Things/Money to Displace anger/rage: termed Sadism, upon our Fellow Man.

AKA the USE of Money to "Throw at our Problems".

(The veritable "Tony Robbins" approach - by a man with over $400 million in financial holdings; or by Oprah, who owned or owns some fifteen homes - palatial ones, at that.)

. . .

As opposed to the use of "Spirituality" as a largely *Alternative* Form of Coping with our Fears - and ultimately, our Fears of Discomforts.

CHAPTER 6

IT TELLS US THAT HAVING EMPATHY IS A MOST "OPTIMAL" WAY OF CONDUCTING LIFE

(AS OPPOSED to the Acquiring of Money and all it provides, including Distractors, Control of Discomforts by way of how it can be used to Structure our Environments and future circumstances - including how and where we might one day live in Old Age, or how much money we may have on hand for a "great lawyer" some day, if ever needed, or for the acquiring of what is termed "potent" Allies (Power, of a sort); or for the purchasing of various Insurances; and for the acquiring of our feeling undue High Regard for ourselves ("grandiosity"), and the Putting Down" of Others - particularly in an effort to injure their Self-Esteem.

Wherein so many are thinking that if only the Above-Mentioned are FIRST acquired, PEOPLE are SUPERFLUOUS: and How one ACQUIRES Good Relations WITH People: NOT through PURCHASING them, but by HAVING EMPATHY FOR them.

. . .

Under the rubric of "To HAVE a Friend, you must first BE a Friend": in other words, one must be able to proffer EMPATHY ("Love"), to HAVE a GENUINE friend - aka spouse or other partner(s), too.

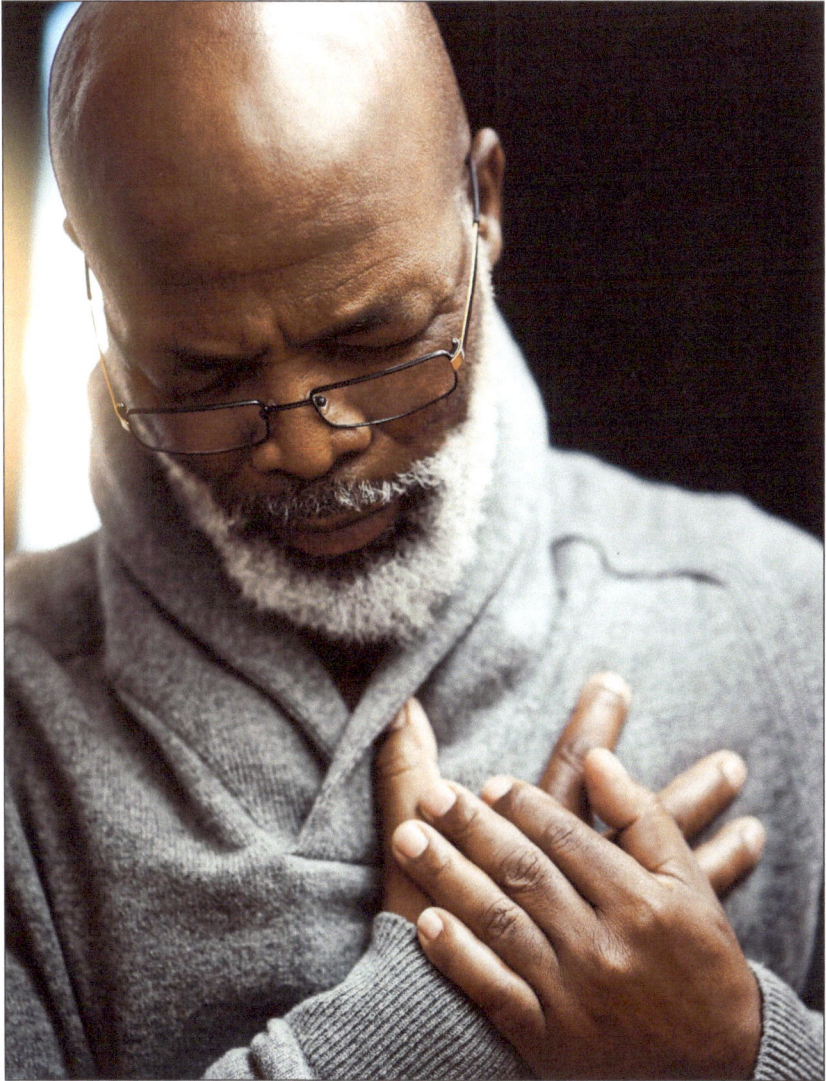

CHAPTER 7

THE VERY SCRIPTURES AND TEACHINGS OF MOST ALL RELIGIONS RARELY EMPHASIZE FOCUSING ON MONEY

(OR IN SHORT, what money almost always is said to bring, even Guarantee):

Security (the absence of Discomforts), Status, and, last but not least, a plethora of Distractors. And even the MEANS of exacting Painful Revenge.

And it often being claimed that IF one HAS a LOT of MONEY, that this MONEY can be USED for PURCHASING. THINGS that will HELP people - "*MATERIALLY*" IMPROVE their LIVES. Or "ENRICH" their lives over all.

To include the bettering of their Physical Health or Longevity.

. . .

Aka "RELIEVE of SUFFERING".

But, are we talking their PHYSICAL suffering, or their EMOTIONAL suffering?

For I would maintain, that providing MONEY for alleviating food shortages, say, or water shortages, or even the correcting of dirty water - to include the building of wells - or war conditions, or housing shortages / issues, or "corrective surgeries" such as the repair of cleft palates, say, or other physical deformities, *or even the extending of one's lifespan* - as defined in physical terms, measured in age spans,

Has LITTLE or NO IMPACT upon the persons' *EMOTIONAL* Suffering, as measured by degree of meaningful SOCIAL CONTACTS; or DEGREE of LOVE (EMPATHY), WITHIN those "contacts" (relationships or interactions); and LITTLE or no IMPACT upon the PROVIDING, thus, of TIME SPENT with a person: CONSISTENTLY - in other words, RELIABLY; and in EMPATHETIC (Understanding) fashion, too; and in, thus, Patient, Uncritical (unblameful) fashion.

It having NO APPRECIABLE IMPACT upon their LEVEL of SELF-ESTEEM; or HOPE level. Or DEGREE of SHAME felt (self-respect).

And this, ULTIMATELY, TOO, NO IMPACT upon their LIFESPAN as measured as BEING ALIVE, EMOTIONALLY.

. . .

(For, consider the words of a famous actor, Anthony Hopkins, that Most people are ZOMBIES.)

Or my contention, that Many People DIED in CHILDHOOD - as per being measured by a great decrease in both Joy and Hope - and then carry on the rest of their lives "living in torpor" - a Shadow of their former Joyful, Playful selves in early childhood:

They are thus living in constant Fear: constant "Danger-Management": and thus HAVING ESSENTIALLY DIED, LONG, LONG AGO for all intents and purposes, and ONLY LIVING a life "DOPED UP", in some fashion - often literally - by their DRUGS of CHOICE - and the Joy-Killing, Thinking-Stultifying, and Growth-Killing SIDE-EFFECTS.

Essentially, on LIFE-SUPPORT. With perhaps an INCREASED LIFESPAN, as measured by PHYSICAL TIME SPENT ON that LIFE SUPPORT, but essentially LONG AGO DEAD: as per Anne Quinlin, say, in the news, long ago: BRAIN-dead, but PHYSI-CALLY, still Alive.

And sadly, our present era - especially in Industrialized Nations, having a Hankering to measure our "Lifespans" NOT in terms of HOW LONG we were alive while NOT BRAIN DEAD, but HOWEVER LONG we EXIST on LIFE SUPPORT, REGARD-LESS of BEING LONG AGO BRAIN- DEAD. (**Or term it a condition of being a "VEGETABLE", or "LOBOTO-MIZED", wherein the MARROW of life, its ESSENCE, is GONE, and we essentially are NO LONGER HUMAN BEINGS.**)

. . .

But instead, a sad DOWNGRADED version of who we INITIALLY STARTED off as being, or had, perhaps, the POTENTIAL to be - under Better conditions....

CHAPTER 8

RELIGION (THEORETICALLY) PROMOTES A LIFESTYLE THAT INCLUDES SOCIAL INTERACTIONS

(AS OPPOSED TO "INTERACTING" with either Objects or Data. Or "drugs".)

At one time, termed "Schizoidism", by American Psychologists, until this became the most commonplace manner of living, whereby this term has gone entirely by the wayside, and is considered even offensive and never used.

CHAPTER 9

IT PROMOTES A WAY OTHER THAN PERFECTIONISM (THEORETICALLY, THAT IS)

WHEREIN, once again, the emphasis on acquiring Understanding, and living, overall, one not just involving Logic - and ensuing obsession with details - but also, the use of "Intuition"; and observing matters, too:

Sometimes deemed the purview of the "Liberal Arts": of Literature, painting, music, and so on.

Or "Right-Brained" Thinking.

Which has the added benefit not just of not focusing so obsessively on a mass of Details - and then having to be concerned with not seeing "The Forest for the Trees", wherein we can start to overlook which particular details are far more important than others - our essentially encountering "Data Smog" - but also, even transcending the use of vocabulary entirely - or downplaying its importance - with the great advantage, too, of escaping whatever built - in biases that any word (term) might have, tied in with its very creation/existence: to include a plethora of words which convey hatred, blame, or other toxic ways of perceiving Reality.

CHAPTER 10

IT PRESENTS A COMPELLING CASE FOR THE BENEFITS OF HAVING SOME FIXED CONSTRAINTS IN OUR LIVES

THESE "CONSTRAINTS" typically termed "Morals", or even Ten Commandments, perhaps, by Christians.

As opposed to governing our lives solely by whatever we might "Feel like, at any given moment - often in turn governed by our sex cravings or our fears, or any anger we may be presently feeling: even feelings of desire for *Revenge,* too.

These Constraints offering us what amount to "Governors" *that cause of to at least Think Twice, before Acting:* acting upon what all too often amount to short-term, or "short-term"-expedient ways of dealing with our impulses.

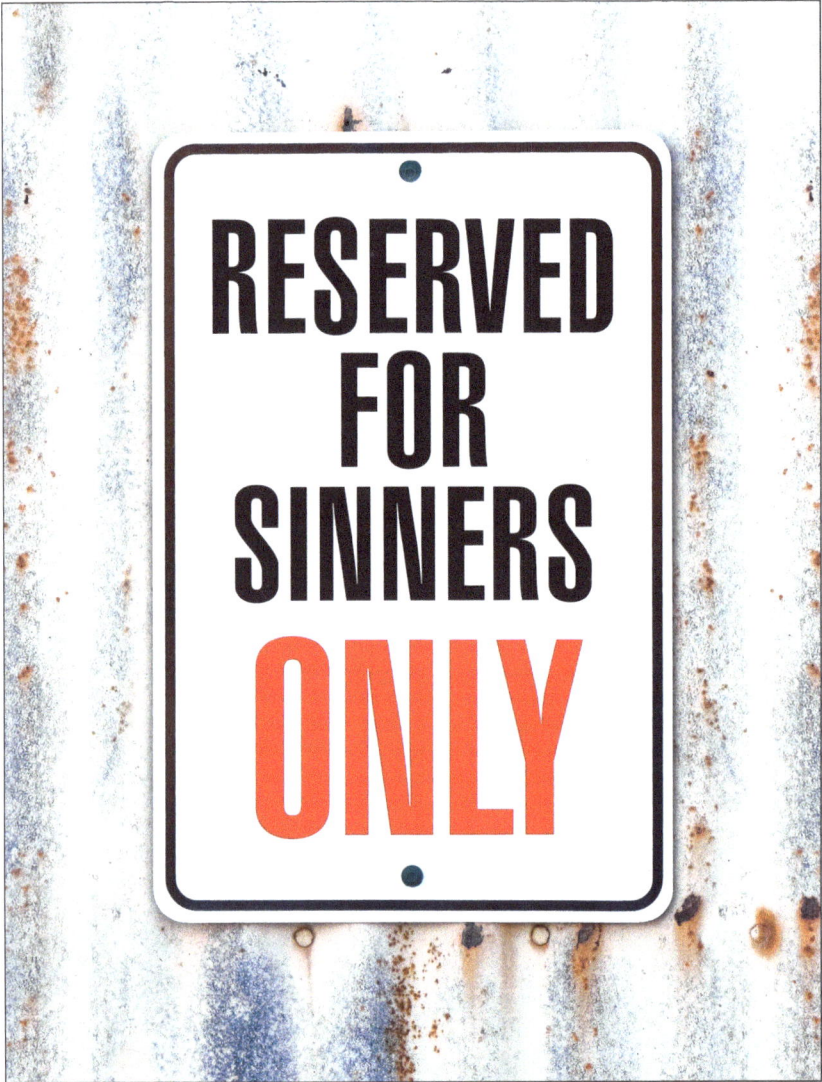

RESERVED FOR SINNERS ONLY

They thus help us govern our lives more by long-term advantages, rather than our following short-term impulses.

Termed "thinking" with our "feelings" only.

. . .

Again, our being, else, driven solely by our Impulses.

CHAPTER 11

RELIGION "DEMOCROTIZES" KNOWLEDGE

IN THAT IT offers all of us, ample Justification to make claim that we can Know - of a sort - Something - about Reality: about how to live life well - and this including how to best seek happiness, and how to size others up, and the ensuing ways to best take care of ourselves in even Old Age, and how to take care of our spouses and children, too:

Without being unduly influenced - or even Dominated - else - by what are alternatively termed "Trained Experts":

Experts, it is said, by way of making claims to being the ONLY persons having the CAPACITY to *SEE* a VARIETY of ASPECTS of *Reality*:

.   .   .

Or, in general, to MAKE ADEQUATE DECISIONS, regarding the best courses of Action to take, concerning a number of matters in Life - and how best to implement such, too.

Not just for one's OWN self - but for one's SPOUSE, say; or one's CHILDREN; or one's NATION; or our PLANET; and finally, for all FUTURE GENERATIONS to come; and ALL SPECIES Upon the EARTH, too; and our EARTH'S ENVIRONMENT.

As opposed to see such partly or greatly with the use of Observation and one's own Logic, and too, the Reviewing of such, and the Discussing of such, with others, and through the use of Scriptural writings and "Spiritual Instruction", in general.

As opposed to being subject to being told that Knowledge of Reality is CONFINED to those to whom it was "Conveyed" by some OTHER source:

Usually, COLLEGE "INSTRUCTION":

(Heralded as More "COMPLETE", and "MORE 'SCIENTIFIC'"", More "OBJECTIVE", and less "SUPERSTITIOUS", and MORE "MODERN".)

.   .   .

(And Created by people who supposedly have "Spent their entire lives focused on this topic or that".)

And who were Supposedly *"Inoculated"* with this Latest "Technology" (Knowledge): and for all time, too: without the need for any refreshing of their memories.

CHAPTER 12

IT PROMOTES NON-GRANDIOSITY - THEORETICALLY

WHEREIN THE CORE IDEA of any and all Religions, is that any and all Humans have FLAWS - such that the Christian Scriptures term us Humans to be "Sinners" - without exception.

And *UNCORRECTABLY* - so, too.

And we are then warned, perhaps, not to Forget this and think ourselves Perfect: "Mini-Gods", if you will: or "narcissists", to use modern parlance.

Both in terms of the false notion of thinking ourselves to either have no flaws, or to have assets which we seemingly Conjured Up out of Thin Air: as if Magicians; or in the notion sometimes used of being a "Self-Made Man" - to include the notion of being termed a "Self-Made Millionaire", or "Pulling Oneself Up by One's Bootstraps".

.   .   .

Of being able to Make things happen out of what amounts to "Spontaneous Combustion": the conjuring up of this or that, once again, Out of Thin Air: without the Requisite Resources or Freedom from any Constraints, if you will.

CHAPTER 13

IT PROMOTES A FEELING OF ACCEPTANCE - AND THUS , WHAT IS TERMED "GRATITUDE"

IT TELLS us we DESERVE NOTHING, and ought ""*ACCEPT WHAT WE GET*":

(**But of course, to also seek out *growth*,** even when it is uncomfortable because it often requires us to face fears we have, or to make some sacrifices in this or that area of our lives.)

Such that we do not simply "rest on our laurels" and claim that we must "accept" whatever we experience in life - without recognizing that some of what makes us who we are - and what we experience in life - what we "get out of life" - has very little to do with such being constrained by our limited lifespan, or the formal schooling that we did or didn't receive - and the quality of it; but rather, has a whole lot more to do with our capacity to "face our fears": one by one, perhaps: instead of conducting a lifetime of running from them, with a variety of "Dodges": whether chemical-based, or other.

(But, at the very same time, not being "hard" on ourselves, such that we "beat ourselves up" for perhaps not ever having made much progress on either the identifying or the reducing of these fears: for it is arguably a gift from a Creator, aka The Universe, to have the requisite resources by which to both see and face those fears - and make real headway on them, thus.)

For this may in fact require not just the Gifts of high intelligence, or lots of "time on one's hands", to Think, and Observe - calmly, slowly, that is - or basically to not just "Do something, but especially, to SIT there": and do what the Christian Scriptures, say, term "Be Still and Know that I am God": or in other words, NOT run around like a chicken with its head cut off, and let certain key Realities of Life, SINK IN: in other words, "Smack oneself UPSIDE the HEAD": wherein one is Given the Gift to SEE what is STARING ONESELF RIGHT IN THE EYE; to SEE What is RIGHT IN FRONT OF ONE'S NOSE."

Wherein, then, having experienced a period of "Carefree" living, as a child, where one was left to "Play" - without being either "micromanaged" by Helicoptering, or not Over-scheduled into a myriad of seemingly beneficial, well-intended "pre-canned", "optimized", vetted "Growth Experiences" - to include "Computer Camp", or Cheerleader Camp - or whatever else we Moderner's have the creativity to either devise or turn into a Money-Making Enterprise, as a "Provider".

. . .

(*This* being more and more *problematic* with the growth of urbanization, wherein many former empty lots and woods once commonplace, fifty years ago, have increasingly been "developed", such that more and more activities must necessarily be conducted on already "owned" property, and this then in turn requiring "permissions" - aka in some "*Program*".)

And also problematic in that, in order to get into the "best schools", it being deemed "necessary" to quantify one's Formative Life Experiences: as per hours attended here or there, in SOME type of "Activity":

Whereas, alternatively, it not being very 'quantifiable", to state that one spent so and so many hours simply be-bopping around one's local area - either on foot or by bike; or spending lots of time at the local swimming hole down at the local river. For how is this easily provable? Who has taken "attendance"? And who is "vetted", too, to do this attendance - taking, such that we even find the tallying "trustworthy"? And finally, who is to say that this experience was "*quality* time"? For perhaps some people did so with "uplifting" child friends; vs others' having done it with other children who would in fact have "dragged them down" - even into juvenile crimes or use of chemical "substances"; and yet others did it with the occasional companionship of rather unusually wise and compassionate adult - friend.

And finally, it even being arguably a Gift, to experience unusually great levels of what some would term "Trauma"; or "Oppression", say - from being "bullied", say, or scapegoated; or subject to being ostracized for some other reason. Or stigmatized - and then, rumors cast about, too. Or perhaps having been born "ugly", of a sort. Or having been born with a physical handicap of sorts; or being an immigrant, or person of a religious Faith which is not of the most "Commonplace" one, in one's Nation or region of their country.

Or to have fallen into a very difficult and costly - in many ways - Addiction.

And a Gift, too, to somehow have grown up or later learned how to Persevere, no matter what: such that, NO MATTER WHAT one PAINFULLY FEELS - no matter HOW MANY times one "FAILS", one "DUSTS ONESELF OFF, and GETS UP and TRIES AGAIN - AND AGAIN - AND AGAIN: to the point that one's relatives and friends might exclaim, "Why don't you just 'Throw in the Towel", and admit Defeat? Are you a "Fool"? Or a "Masochist": a person who seeming ENJOYS feeling unending pain?"

Such that this - *despite* all the painful emotions suffered in life - whether hunger, or loss of property, or losses in relationships or loved ones' very lives, or injuries sustained; or imprisonment, say, or one or more periods of "homelessness", and considerable "unpredictabilities" in Life, which many would shudder at - one nevertheless NEVER GIVES UP HOPE: Hope that Something Might Just CHANGE: *SOMEHOW*.

Which thus is a GIFT, TOO: **the Gift of NOT DESPAIRING;** of NOT GIVING UP; or of not GIVING IN to feelings of PANIC - and turning to drug use, say; or non-empathetic activities - aka "Using

Others"; or of NOT "SELLING OUT" in terms of how one garners money, too - that is, by Altering one's Moral Code, so as to make the making either of Money or Friendships, or even garnering a Marriage Partner, far easier.

And also have to face comments such as: "What makes you think you CAN even OVERCOME what you are TRYING to overcome - and ultimately ACHIEVE? What makes You think YOU can SUCCEED, when FEW OTHERS CAN?"

"Do You thus 'Think You are Special'?"

——

And thus, the alternative to feeling angry over one's Circumstances, arguably termed "Feeling *Grateful*".

Wherein then, this tending to produce the very ironic situation of a person who is seeming deemed to be "Understandably" Suffering - by all conventional Societal standards - even if suffering by way of being Enslaved or considered "Dirt Poor" - or deemed to be "Oppressed" - subject to Enslavement, say, and then also, again, financially poor, and having severe Restrictions as to their Liberties to move about as they desire.

And yet, IF possessing *HOPE* - in other words, *not* filled with Bitterness (chronic anger) and a desire to blame, and even to seek revenge - this person then being deemed *LUCKY*: and even regarded with "ENVY": for quite possibly, it is the HAVING of HOPE - of GROWTH BEING POSSIBLE - which is the GREATEST ASSET POSSIBLE to "POSSESS", in life.

. . .

And it arguably being the LACK of Hope - of anything ever

CHANGING - of change being "statistically" POSSIBLE - which is the greatest "cause" of Mankind's happiness: and why, likely, why the United States is in a three-way tie for the greatest per capita use of "Antidepressant drugs, despite our greater degree of "Material" affluence, and our terming ourselves "lucky" to not be a "Third World" nation or "Developing Nation".

For, perhaps if measured using the "yardstick" of How much HOPE we have, the average American has so little, compared to many other nations, that we are arguably not simply a "Third World" nation, but a "TENTH World" Nation.

Indeed, carried to its logical conclusion, one might ask, just *HOW WEALTHY* a person IS to be CONSIDERED, *IF "Living"* IN a COFFIN, ENCRUSTED with MANY JEWELS, and emplaced in a MAGNIFICENT CRYPT, too: but yet, DEAD? "Deader than a Doornail", when it comes to the CAPACITY to EXPERIENCE GREAT HAPPINESS? IF one is simply EXISTING - trying to "KILL TIME", before one's PHYSICAL death?

Or to put it another way, does it MATTER to us, to be considered to have IMMENSE *FINANCIAL* or *MATERIAL* Wealth, DURING the periods of time in which we are ASLEEP?

And then - by asleep, I mean not just Physiologically asleep, but **arguably "*EMOTIONALLY*" asleep: ASLEEP in terms of the DEGREE of HAPPINESS we are consistently experiencing:**

. . .

(Wherein, *isn't the Operational definition* of being even *PHYSIOLOGICALLY* asleep, that we *EXPERIENCE* very *LITTLE?*)

Very little consistent *Joy*, in short: we are essentially "ZONED OUT": (Unless constantly experiencing highly pleasurable Dreams?). Or, that we experience NIGHTMARES? (Periods of Great Fears.)

(Hence the title of a book, on the excessive use of Psychiatric drugs, entitled "Comfortably Numb"; and the term "Spaced Out"; or "Strung Out"; or being "Stoned"; or "lobotomized".)

Yes, IF a person is not experiencing a whole lot of Joy, and instead feeling chronic anger and fears (aka "worries", if tied to commonplace fears tied to money or one's job or possessions), then isn't this akin to experiencing - at best - no more than what someone who's brain has been sliced-and-diced by a surgeon, to effect Calmness - and termed a Lobotomy?????

═══

FOR does it *MATTER*, to one's *Happiness* - level, whether one is *ASLEEP* upon a BED which is valued at $10,000 - and whether this bed is located within a "home" with a value of TEN MILLION Dollars?

As opposed to being asleep upon a straw mat, and this, in a cave or barn, or on a boat?

. . .

Or whether one **wearing Gucci or Armani pajamas** - or simply sweat pants or gym shorts?

Rather than what is termed "COMPLAINING" ("Belly-aching"), over what we THINK we DESERVED but DIDN'T GET.

(Including any economic "disparities", or what is connoted by the phrase "I Got the Short End of the Stick".)

Or even, in a certain way of looking at it, the claim made that it is "Unfair" that "I had a so-called 'ABUSIVE' Childhood.

But Rarely - outside of the Religious perspective, is there a truthful ACKNOWLEDGEMENT that NOT EVEN the EXISTENCE of the UNIVERSE - is "OWED" us.

Or, that we were ever even CONCEIVED. Or not ABORTED.

Or, born as a HUMAN - and NOW - vs a. FRUITFLY or MAYFLY or COW: and thus, NOT in CAVE MAN days, too - where life expectancy was on the order of twenty-five years, say.

But whereas the NON-Religious Perspective is one of "I *DESERVE*" this and that. And a concomitant FIGHTING mentality, the Minute we deem ourselves HAVING LESS than ANYONE ELSE:

.   .   .

(Their myopically not SEEING, that ON SOME DISTANT PLANETS, the LIFESPAN of a "human" might be TEN THOUSAND years, and that THEIR favorite leisure activity might involve "taking a spin" to a local, nearby PLANET, for a "bite to eat".)

And thus, all "bellyaching" being utterly WITHOUT WARRANT, in the overall picture of things.

(Aside: when was the last time we ever heard a COW or CHICKEN COMPLAIN, that IT did NOT GET ITS FAIR SHARE? To GET to BE a HUMAN BEING, on PLANET EARTH, and IN TODAY'S TIME?)

CHAPTER 14

AND TO REITERATE: RELIGIONS DO NOT INVALIDATE THE EXPERIENCES OF "TINY PEOPLE

YES, RELIGIONS "DEMOCRATIZE" the VALID CLAIM, that UNDERSTANDING of the ESSENTIALS of Life, is NOT the PURVIEW of ONLY a SELECT FEW - to whom supposed "SPE-CIAL TRAINING" was CONFERRED or AVAILED of - namely, a "VETTED" COLLEGE-TRAINING PROGRAM.

BUT INSTEAD, is OBTAINABLE or CONFERRED by OTHER MEANS, too - if not EXCLUSIVELY SO, perhaps: to include:

Our UPBRINGING: whether ones involving LOTS of EMPATHY shown.

And LIFE EXPERIENCES.

· · ·

(The more varied, the better, and the MORE NOT FORGOTTEN, too, the better; and THE MOST WELL-PERCEIVED, the better - wherein a life of varied experiences, gone through in RUSHED, HELTER-SKELTER Fashion, being hardly WELL-PONDERED or WELL-ASSIMILATED (REMEMBERED, for the LONG-Term.)

And the NATURE of the MORAL CODES one was TAUGHT, or NOT, in one's Childhood; and modeled, by some, too.

And the EMPHASIS - or not - upon MONEY - *what it DOES or doesn't do* - for a person - in one's childhood.

And the degree of FREE TIME one HAD, as a child.
    Versus being Shuffled from one "Enrichment Program" to another.
    And the degree of "Helicopter-Parenting" involved.

And issues of whether one attended Day Care or not - wherein Care was then provided by a 20-year-old "Rent-a-Parent", who is paid minimum wage, and has to cope with the "raising" of a number of children all at once.

And the NUMBER and DEGREE of HARDSHIPS experienced, in one's life:

.   .   .

Where, IF it is "IN the Cards", one HAS the TIME and ENERGY and BRAINPOWER and STAMINA to SORT OUT what CAN be LEARNED from such: the SILVER LININGS, if you will.

Hence the phrase "NO PAIN, NO GAIN."

And how STEEL is FORGED, out of IRON, though FIRE.

And, in general, how DIFFICULTIES HOPEFULLY cause us to CLARIFY our THOUGHTS - on our EXPE-RIENCES, our PHILOSOPHY of LIFE, and PEOPLE in general: including WHAT "MAKES THEM (and ourselves) TICK."

This sometimes being referred to as the Acquiring of a Degree - perhaps a "Ph.D", or two or five or ten of them - from the Greatest University on the Planet, some would say: The University of the School of Hard Knocks.

.   .   .

Which tends to especially train us not in superfluous trivialities, but in WHAT makes us *HAPPIEST* in Life: as HUMAN BEINGS.

CHAPTER 15

THE CASE OF CULTS...

SURELY, every person has their own definition of what a "cult" is or isn't, as applied too, to the topic of Religions. These are my thoughts at the present time, on "cults":

First, I would state that I believe that all religions are not perfect - that there is, in every religion, some one or more aspects that could be "better".

In other words, that religions are like people - and thus, relationships: each is a "compromise solution" to living life: wherein we "adopt" the "use" of a person or religion because we believe we will be better off with such, overall, than without it - at least for the present time....

However, it being true, surely, that there are some religions which have far too many "negative" aspects to them, and their "plus" elements either not that significant, or else, the "negatives" are simply what I would term "too 'toxic'", to offset the positives....

SUCH religions, as we say, sometimes, about people, too, I would term "TOXIC RELIGIONS": OR, for short, ""*CULTS*".

—

Now, what, in my opinion, would I consider an element that would make for a "toxic" religion - or so, for some persons - and thus, qualify as a "Cult", at least for some? Here are some thoughts of mine....

A. The Religion is used to Enhance the Power of the Leader - the creator of that Religion: but, more specifically, to the *detriment* of the *followers*.

One might term such, a "narcissistic" religious leader - and, if only aggrandizing themselves, this termed "healthy" narcissism; but, if the self-aggrandizing is accompanied by "putting others down", too, such being quite injurious to some - to those, say, with low self-esteem, or for those who are easily swayed to believe whatever others say, to include what is incorrectly said, about theirselves.

B. The Religion states that one is a "Lowly Worm".

(And, moreover, that if so, that one is a "Lowly Worm" out of "Choice', not because one was either Created that way, or Evolved to be so.)

And furthermore, any Religion which states, too, that all persons are equally Lowly: both Adolph Hitler, thus, vs. Mother Teresa, or Gandhi, say; or your mother, vs. the veritable image brought up by the term "Axe-murderer".

.   .   .

C. Any Religion which exists solely to Make Money. And especially egregious, if this money-making has toxic side-effects upon others: upon the followers, that is.

Wherein the Religion, in my view, ought first and foremost, as "Doing No Harm", at least. That it thus be no more harmful than a "sugar pill" - a placebo; or a glass of water, say.

D. Any Religion which garners its "converts" through clear - or not so clear - threats.

To include, threats that cannot easily be "dealt with", by either easily complying with the "Requirements" necessary to not be harmed; or too, threats wherein the Criteria for such "Compliance" are so murky, that one never is quite sure, from day to day, where one stands, in terms of "making the grade", so as not to garner such Punishment.

D. Any Religion - and its leaders - which asks a person to "end their life": case in point, Jim Jones' group, "Jonestown", in Guyana:

James Warren Jones (May 13, 1931 – November 18, 1978) was an American cult leader, political activist, preacher, and faith healer who led the Peoples Temple, a new religious organization which existed between 1955 and 1978. In what he described as "revolutionary suicide", Jones and his inner circle orchestrated a mass murder–suicide in his remote jungle commune at Jonestown, Guyana, on November 18, 1978.

· · ·

Following a period of negative media publicity and reports of abuse at Peoples Temple, Jones ordered the construction of a commune called Jonestown in Guyana in 1974, and convinced or compelled many of his followers to live there with him. Jones claimed that he was constructing a socialist paradise free from the oppression of the United States government. By 1978, media reports had surfaced of human rights abuses and accusations that people were being held in Jonestown against their will. U.S. Representative Leo Ryan led a delegation to the commune in November of that year to investigate these reports. While boarding a return flight with some former Temple members who had wished to leave, Ryan and four others were murdered by gunmen from Jonestown. Jones then ordered a mass murder-suicide that claimed the lives of 909 commune members, 304 of them children; almost all of the members died by drinking Flavor Aid laced with cyanide."

https://en.wikipedia.org/wiki/Jim_Jones

(As of March 7th, 2022).

E. Any Religion which has the effect of inculcating shame or guilt - and, without a reliable means, too, of solving this shame or guilt.

F. Any Religion which states that some people are "better" than other people.

(In this sense, I would consider the idea, of Adolph Hitler, as to some being Superior to others, and his overall concept, then, of a "Master Race", to be Toxic, and thus, a Cult, of sorts.)

This would also be the case, I would say, for any Religion that says that one is "Sub-Human" based on level of financial holdings, say. Or

Ethnic origin, once again, or level of "intelligence" - however one is to try to measure such; or skin color; or gender.

G. Any Religion where the Leader claims to have key information from "Divine Intervention", but is unable to definitively prove this. And moreover, that the Leader of this Religion then states that he or she has, thus, the necessary "criteria" to be considered "Correct" - without any further scrutiny.

H. Any Religion which does not have, as a Central Tenet, certain core values that include Respect for all persons; and Respect for Life; or which try to justify the taking of others' lives in a claim that it is "necessary" for "Self-Defense" - without discussing, say, just what the criteria for how many it would be justifiable to see either die or be "enslaved", in the seeking of this "Self-Defense".

To put this another way, if it were stated, in the Religion, that it is "ok" to take the life of another person, in certain cases, "in 'Self-Defense'", then what about the taking of five lives, for this? Or two hundred? Or the lives of an entire other nation, or the entire Planet, even? ... To save the life of one? And for how long is this "defended" person to even live longer, and to whose benefit? Just their own bene-fit, or the benefit of a few others? Or many, many others? How many others? And how will they benefit? By the indulging in sheer plea-sures? Or by something of more value?

I. Any Religion which greatly"highlights" the value of Love, but which defines "Love" only in terms of "DOING things", either for the Leader, or for others; but which does not discuss the more important - in this author's opinion - issue of defining Love as Acceptance, first and foremost.

And by "acceptance", I mean, the concept that every person, as a part of a Universe which follows Laws of cause and effect, cannot possibly be "held 'Responsible'", in any way, shape or form, for what they cannot "help" doing: they cannot thus be "held responsible" for finding a way to break those Laws of the Universe; in other words the breaking of the Laws of Cause and Effect.

And thus, that no human being can be "held responsible" for "transcending", without adequate means, the limitations, by way of cause and effect, that their human body imposes: in terms of having a limited lifespan, say; and by way of having limited time for self-growth; and having a limited capacity for remembering things; and having susceptibility to both fear and rage or anger - by way of having an Amygdala as part of one's brain; and because one has a built-in "craving" for self-survival, and thus, procreating of their existence - which then means having a "sex drive", and all that follows, in seeking the satisfying of such; and because their bodies are rather frail, some more so than others; and because they are of limited intelligence, to include not being able to "read the minds" of others. And because they cannot easily or completely transfer what they have learned, by the time they die, to either their offspring or others in general; and because they know they will one day die — often preceded by painful illness; and this then producing immense stress upon the person; and because they see others die, including loved ones near and dear - and this being very stressful. And because they have to spend time on many rather mundane matters for mere "maintenance" of their lives or the lives of their loved ones, leaving quastionable time left for self-growth or the aiding of anyone else, too.

CHAPTER 16

THE CURIOUS ISSUE OF RELIGIOUS TRAUMA... WHY SOME ARE STRONGLY TRAUMATIZED BY CERTAIN RELIGIONS - AND OTHERS, NOT THE LEAST...

THE TOPIC of Religious Trauma is somewhat complicated, surely, with differing viewpoints, but these are ideas I presently see merit in:

First, that it is rather like a soldier returning from a battlefield: wherein the person suffering greatly afterward, emotionally - "traumatized", if you will, might have a few key distinguishing "features":

First of all, they are far more "empathic" in nature, than those who do *not* "develop" trauma.

In fact, for those soldiers who actually enjoyed ending the lives of others on a battlefield - in other words, enjoyed killing either an enemy or anyone at all - would surely never "suffer" "trauma".

Second, it strikes me, that in terms of Religious "trauma", that this person so "afflicted", would *not* be the person is of a "manner", whereby they deem themselves "perfect" - what one might term somewhat "grand" in how they."view" theirselves, then this person would surely believe that they fall into a "Special Category", where being Assessed by a Religion's Leader - or Deity - is concerned: to include in matters of "Judgement about matters concerning Eternity...."

For if they are (rather) "perfect" already, then they are in essence gods or goddesses already, and thus, exempt from the criteria that is being used to "assess" - to "judge" - others.

Additionally, as a sort of corollalry, such would no be the type who, if they don't deem themselves perfect, *do* believe they are essentially "good enough"...

   because they have a certain number of friends, or have had such, over the years, such that they are not deeming themselves "unlovable" by the entire human race, then this is a far different situation than for those who have never had any friends at all, or only one, say; or who have never been able to go on dates, say, or marry, despite desiring to, and also trying mightily, to do so.

Such persons might have found themselves "shunned" by way of being "ugly", or not of the same level of aggressiveness as those around them; or envied, for some reason, by a great many; or too "shy" by way of excessive fears; or perhaps they played no sports, if a male, in America; or, were not "wearing the right clothing"; or had a different sexual "orientation" than most all others; or perhaps, their religious views or precepts, or their parents, had prohibited either sexual "activities", to include dating, or whatever else. To even include the mere pleasures of seeing another person of the opposite gender, say - or what have you; and this tied, too, to just how "promiscuous" a culture they were in, and how they fit into this, in general.

Third, if a person - or soldier - has no emotional supports, in life, this person surely will suffer more, from any type of difficulty in general.

Fourth, if the person has no "access" to ways of Coping - call such Defense Mechanisms, if you will - and "emotional supports" being one such type of Defense Mechanism - then surely, this person will suffer more, and may be termed "traumatized" - when in fact, the person simply does not have "access" to a Way of Coping: a Defense Mechanism;

Perhaps because their religious views prohibit the use of such; or their high level of empathy, too, precludes such; or, they may not have the necessary income level to purchase any number of Ways of Coping; or, they may not be "beautiful"or "handsome", and so, right here, too, unable to obtain certain Ways of Coping that would be available to many others; or maybe they cannot obtain work - or at a suitable level of income, and sufficient degree of suitability in general ; or too, they may not "fit" into their culture in certain ways, either ethnically, or in terms of being of equal intelligence; or they may have a different view on money or love or sexuality.

CHAPTER 17

A BRIEF DEPARTING COMMENT...

MY BRIEF, brief comment about Religion in general, is this:

If it does not serve your overall happiness, then perhaps it is not a Religion - but a Tool - for someone else's benefit.

And might need "looking into": might well bear close scrutiny, in days to come.

ACKNOWLEDGMENTS

All photos - unless identified otherwise - are provided by Canva. Cover photo by Amazon.

ABOUT THE AUTHOR

The author would welcome your thoughts.... At the email of dolphinskylines@gmail.com.

Author in 2021

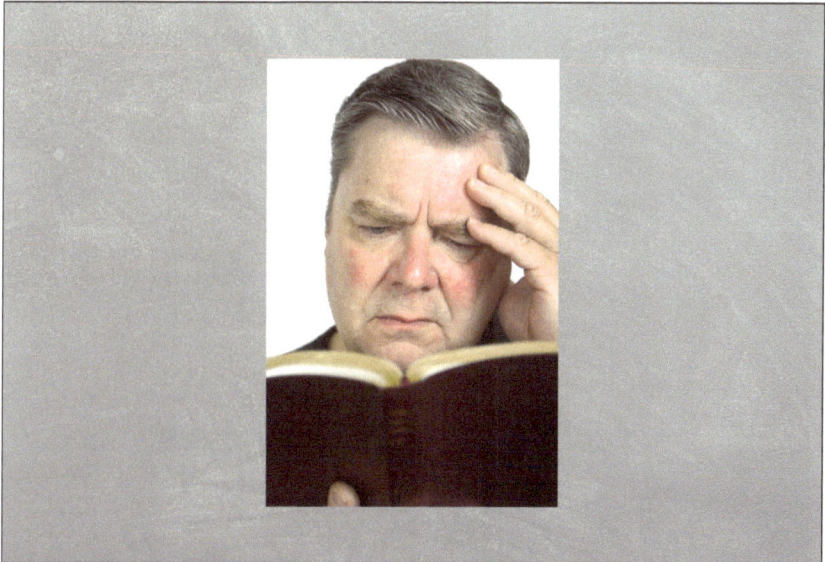

Surely we need to Hang in there, with our Search for Truth - for
What is Best, right? For if Life were easy to figure out at all, and
even All Knowable to us mere Mortals, wouldn't we be Gods, and
maybe quite bored, too?